M000311711

EFT and Tapping
for Beginners
The Essential EFT Manual to Start Relieving Stress,
Losing Weight, and Healing

Rockridge Press

TABLE OF CONTENTS

INTRODUCTION

Is your life filled with more stress and pressure than fun? Your job, family, academics, money worries—even traffic jams and supermarket lines—may make you want to scream with frustration at times. Perhaps every single day seems to consist of nothing but deadlines you have to meet. Do you feel as if somehow, somewhere, you got lost along the way?

We all have fears, concerns, insecurities, and possibly phobias that prevent us from reaching our full potential . . . and accumulated daily stress only makes it worse. More intimidating. Less controllable. Life becomes overwhelming.

Now there's a way to help you heal and manage life for the better. Your goals, hopes, and dreams become more attainable because you are more positive and motivated. You move forward with clarity and confidence for one simple reason: you feel better. You are healthier and far more positive.

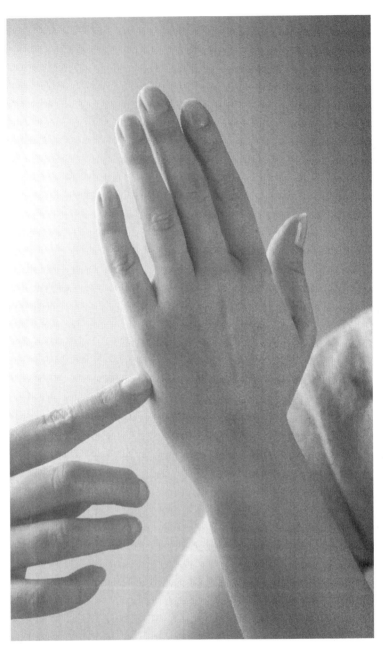

The main tapping points are easy to learn.

If that sounds too good to be true, welcome to the benefits of tapping, or Emotional Freedom Technique (EFT). Tapping is a holistic three-in-one therapy you can do anytime, anywhere, at no cost, and without drugs. Tapping is a natural way of accessing and easing the emotional or medical issues that negatively impact you. You feel better. You take back control of your life. Life is fun again.

Tapping combines the principles of meditation, positive affirmations, and acupressure on meridian points of your body to help release energy blockages from the affected areas. Sound a bit esoteric? Not at all, when you think about it. Acupuncture has been central to Chinese medicine for thousands of years; everything from massage to acupressure is based on exactly the same principles.

The Centers for Disease Control and Prevention (CDC) estimates that 85 percent of disease is caused by emotion; that's why "a positive attitude is crucial to healing." By healing the emotional causes for the disease, you very often heal the physical body.

The ever-increasing interest in holistic healing is based on the realization that for every pill prescribed to treat a condition, a host of other medications are needed to offset the side effects of the original cure. For every pill swallowed, immunities build up and dosages increase. At best, physical dependency is the result. Too often a mental and emotional dependency is as well.

Can something as simple as tapping preclude a need for a plethora of drugs? In many cases, yes. Tapping is truly a holistic approach to healing and to maintaining good health.

EFT was originally designed to overhaul the psychotherapy profession. Fortunately, that goal has been reached as EFT has dramatically reduced therapy time from months or years down to minutes or hours.

Along the way, we kept noticing that profound physical healings were also taking place. Vision improved, headaches disappeared, cancer pains and symptoms subsided, and so on. . . . EFT addresses causes that Western Healing Practices have largely ignored. Medicine, for example, pays very little attention to disruptions in the body's energy meridians nor does it give much weight to emotional causes. These causes, of course, are the centerpiece of EFT.

Gary Craig, *The EFT Manual* (2011)

In this book, we'll be taking a look at various aspects of tapping—from brain mapping to meditation, from acupuncture to chiropractic. Nothing is highly technical, but sources are included if you want greater depth of knowledge. We've included some easy-to-follow directions on how to tap, as well.

This book is not intended to replace your medical program. Tapping can never set a broken bone or inoculate against polio, smallpox, or tetanus. Tapping can, however, put an end to your reliance on medication to get up in the morning and go to sleep at night. Tapping can make your life more fun, more positive, and much healthier. Tapping can make you feel better mentally, emotionally, and physically.

1

WHAT IS TAPPING?

The last fifty years has seen the "birth" of tapping as a tool in both psychological and medical treatment protocols. It was in the mid-1960s that Dr. George Goodheart, working within the field of applied kinesiology, first began using acupressure in lieu of acupuncture. A decade later, Australian psychiatrist John Diamond, MD, included affirmations to treat emotional problems, and behavioral kinesiology came into being.

Enter the American psychologist Dr. Roger Callahan. He combined applied and behavioral kinesiologies and incorporated the meridian system of acupuncture as a method to aid in the treatment of his patients who suffered from anorexia, phobias, and anxiety disorders. By the 1980s, Callahan had combined "tapping" for emotional problems with concurrently focusing on the problem to be resolved. Quite accidentally, he discovered that if a person focused on a specific fear at the time of tapping, that fear could be removed. And thus Thought Field Therapy (TFT) was born.

Gary Craig, who had studied under Dr. Callahan, developed the single-algorithm approach we know as Emotional Freedom Technique (EFT) in the early 1990s. Craig's approach transformed tapping into an easily acquired self-administered tool for the layperson. There was no longer a need to tap on the exact spots, nor did the user have to understand in detail the underlying muscular and meridian structure. Craig brought the EFT practice into the mainstream because he developed a way to make it understandable and doable for the general population.

What's Ahead for EFT?

Patricia Carrington, PhD, has predicted that EFT will soon become widespread due to its potential for treating challenging conditions that would otherwise be drawn out. She states that:

> EFT (Emotional Freedom Technique) is now the most influential and widely known Energy Psychology method in the world. It is being incorporated into psychological treatment protocols for traumas as well as for many other emotional problems previously considered treatable only by lengthy and usually only partially effective procedures.
>
> (Patricia Carrington, n.d.)

The Origins of Tapping

You might have heard about remarkable health improvements from tapping or read about someone turning his or her life around from an emotional perspective, but the odds are you're reading this book because you're relatively new to the concept of tapping.

Yes, tapping is a recent practice, but it's grounded in the principles of acupuncture with the understanding that pressure on various points of the body stimulates a corresponding and specific area of the brain. As such, tapping is deeply rooted in 5,000-year-old Chinese acupuncture practices—but without the needles. Here's to modern-day thinking!

The central premise for both tapping and acupuncture is the same: health issues are caused by the blockage of proper energy flow along various meridian points to the brain. Stimulation of specific trigger points release that blocked energy, and then healing begins.

The difference between tapping and acupuncture is that acupuncture addresses purely physical problems, whereas tapping addresses emotional issues as well. Remember the Centers for Disease Control and Prevention (CDC) statistic that approximately 85 percent of all illness is caused by acknowledged or unacknowledged negative emotions? In the proverbial nutshell, tapping is emotional or psychological acupuncture.

Tapping can help alleviate health issues, which will be discussed in greater depth later. But it is important for anyone considering the practice of tapping to truly understand

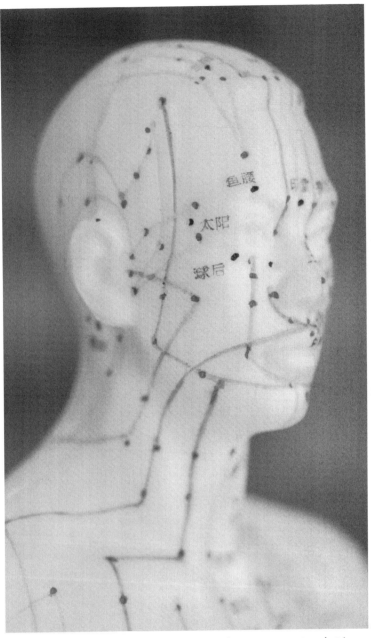

Tapping accesses many of the same energy points as acupuncture but is greatly simplified, and it doesn't use needles!

that the central focus of the method is on the release of negative emotions.

To be effective, tapping should be incorporated into daily life. Those negative emotions didn't just arrive at your mind's door one day. Certainly, an event might have triggered the initial distrust, fear, or pain, but years of living with that nemesis has buried it and allowed subsequent events and emotions to add layers of protective "scar tissue." That is what ultimately causes the blockage of proper energy flow.

The reason for daily tapping sessions is maintenance—you want to keep positive energy flowing regularly. Issues or concerns can change; it is the actual touching of pressure points and positive affirmations (which can differ based on your needs at any specific time) that keeps your mind and body functioning at its peak.

Tapping is very much a practice and a process that improves all aspects within your life. Performed daily, it allows your energy to flow freely and serves as a mainstay for positive health in all aspects. In this sense, tapping is no different from yoga, Pilates, tai chi, or any other form of stretching or focused breathing and concentrated effort intended to keep you in optimal health. You don't stretch only when your back aches; you stretch daily to prevent backaches and resulting injuries, such as sciatic nerve damage.

Tapping is not psychology as Western medicine defines the term. Tapping does not require you to go back and mentally or emotionally discover and dissect the cause to hopefully resolve the problem. Instead, unblocking your energy flow washes away the negative, or what lies at the bottom of what you want to address. When you can do this, healing begins.

In a way, it involves much the same principle as when you cut yourself. The natural bleeding process removes the germs from the kitchen knife that caused the cut. Of course, you also wash your cut with hydrogen peroxide and use an antiseptic ointment to speed up healing, but the body's initial response of bleeding is what cleans the wound of potential infection. So too, tapping helps rid the body of the "germs" of negative energy, supporting and enhancing other traditional healing methods.

2

WHAT CAN TAPPING DO FOR YOU?

Before answering this question, let's take a brief look at the three best-known methods of dealing with emotional turmoil and insecurities. This will give you a better understanding of where tapping fits in with treatment and why it works. You will quickly spot similarities between tapping and the other disciplines.

Three general methods are used to deal with issues that confront and sometimes frighten us. All three are intended to help find balance and perspective. All are effective. All are contingent on an individual's ability to open up, to stick with it, and—in the case of formal therapy, counseling, and some mentoring—to be able to afford the incurred costs.

To deal with emotional and physical concerns, there are a few processes we are all aware of.

Freewriting and journaling are effective ways to clarify your thoughts and decide on achievable goals.

Free Writing and Journaling

Free writing and journaling (or keeping a diary) is used most often as a means to express thoughts and emotions. The premise has always been that to write them down—to see the actual words in black and white in your own handwriting—is to acknowledge the reality of internal turmoil and conflict, and to subsequently gain some clarity and objectivity about it.

Journaling is used for everything from tracking the food you eat, to helping determine your relationship values, to uncovering strengths and interests related to career choices and paths. This method is completely at no cost to the writer, but it does require some diligence in sticking with it. While journaling greatly helps release pent-up emotions and frustrations, perhaps the most important results include clarity and perspective.

Formal Therapy or Counseling

Formal therapy or counseling run the gamut from treating serious disorders to helping people learn to deal with everyday issues. These practices attempt to treat everything from panic attacks to addiction, from suicidal tendencies to normal rebellion, from general antipathy to severe psychosis. That's one reason why specialists dealing in this area have titles ranging from psychiatrist, to psychoanalyst, to licensed social worker.

For most of us, the term *counseling* implies that less-severe issues are involved, although this may not always be the case. Counseling is, however, more or less interpreted as just that: guidance and counseling.

There is a growing adjunct to this classification—that of mentoring. Mentoring is more of a give-and-take, one-on-one discovery process than is either formal therapy or counseling. The rapid growth of mentoring by licensed social workers, especially in the cases of teenage angst and by business coaches for career decisions, is testimony to the fact that people do benefit from talking things out when given the knowledge and courage to see themselves clearly and to vocalize aspirations honestly and without fear of condemnation.

Talking with Friends and Family

Talking through an issue with a friend or family member is a common way to share feelings, concerns, and frustrations—we've all done it. And talking it out is healthy. One problem with talking it out, however, is that the other person may well be hurt by what you have to say. Perhaps past conversations made them feel bad, insecure, or rejected. As much as we love our friends and family, that simple fact does temper our honesty toward them and theirs toward us.

Communication—effective communication—is vital to any healthy relationship, and it's something we should strive for in all our interactions. Yet talking it out fails when the person you're talking to is not—cannot be—totally objective, because they, too, are directly involved in the situation. This presents a bit of a conundrum, and it can inhibit you from sharing your thoughts completely.

Tapping as an Alternative Approach

First, suspend any questions and possible disbelief. Tapping does work. You should also accept that a certain amount of patience is required. You might feel a wash of relief after your first attempt; you might only feel a twinge. Everyone is different and as individual and unique as the issues needing to be addressed.

Now be honest with the next step. What emotional, mental, or physical issues do you want to address and eliminate? Write them down the left column of a piece of paper. Seeing your list of concerns helps you to be more serious about making your life better.

Next to the "I Want to Eliminate" column, write down what you want to achieve. The following table gives you some examples.

I Want to Eliminate	I Want to Achieve
STRESS	Calmness
	Perspective on my life
	Better judgment
	Improved sleep
JOB FRUSTRATION	Clarity
	Better judgment
	Reduced stress
MIGRAINE HEADACHES	No pain
	Physical health
	Better sleep
RELATIONSHIP PROBLEMS	Love
	Closeness
	Joy
	Companionship
	Fun
EXCESS WEIGHT	A fitter body
	Better health
	More energy
	More confidence

Are you seeing the crossover in some of the "I Want to Achieve" lists? That's because so many of these emotional and physical negatives are tied together. When one part of your life is off track, it impacts many facets, causing physical and emotional reactions in other areas.

By creating a list of improvements specific to your situation and desires, you are taking the first step toward a better life with the help of tapping.

3

WHAT TAPPING
CAN HELP YOU CONQUER

This chapter summarizes some primary issues that tapping has helped people overcome. You'll find more specific details on each of these concerns, along with information and examples of success in other areas, in later chapters. None of the following issues may apply to you, or more than a few might. What is important to remember is that these problems impact more than one area of your life. There are very definite crossovers of "symptoms" within the primary nomenclature used to describe each one. This section is intended solely to help you identify what you might be feeling, as well as gain an understanding of the range of concerns that tapping can help you banish.

Common Problems

Stress

Stress is simply a reaction to a stimulus that disturbs a person's physical or mental equilibrium. It is your body's way of reacting to a challenge. Stress describes a condition that can have an impact, usually negatively, on your mental and physical well-being.

The practice of tapping allows blocked energy to flow freely throughout your system, thus eliminating many of the causes and symptoms of stress.

Anxiety

Anxiety is a mood—an unpleasant state of inner turmoil. It's often accompanied by nervous behavior, fatigue, muscular tension, and difficulty sleeping.

The practice of tapping allows energy to flow freely throughout your system and eliminates many of the causes and symptoms of anxiety.

Depression

The Mayo Clinic has stated that depression is "different from normal sadness in that it engulfs your day-to-day life, interfering with your ability to work, study, eat, sleep, and have fun." And that "feelings of helplessness, hopelessness, and worthlessness are intense and unrelenting, with little, if any, relief."

Overcoming pain, both physical and emotional, is why tapping was created.

The process of tapping has proven beneficial in easing the symptoms of depression for many people; however, we strongly recommend you first discuss the practice of tapping with your doctor if your depression is severe or if you are on prescription drugs as part of your treatment.

Pain Management

Pain management can run the gamut from physical therapy, to prescription drugs, to acupuncture, and yes, to tapping. If you are suffering from pain, whether temporary or long term, the practice of tapping can help mitigate your suffering. Pain management very often incorporates acupuncture and chiropractic treatments, and tapping is a daily practice that enhances and maintains what is achieved with both.

Weight Loss

Eating disorders (overeating, binge eating, and anorexia) are emotional habits and reactions to stressful or unhappy situations. Excess weight, extreme body-consciousness resulting in anorexia, or yo-yoing weight can lead to the onset of diabetes, heart concerns, and any number of emotional and psychological issues.

Because most eating disorders are centered around an emotional issue, addressing the specific issue through tapping is a proven path to healthy weight loss, maintenance of a proper weight, and a long-term healthy diet regimen.

Blood Pressure

Blood pressure is the force of blood flowing through your arteries. According to the National Heart, Lung, and Blood Institute, "if this pressure rises and stays high over time, it can damage the body in many ways" (n.d.). About one-third of adults in the United States have high blood pressure, but because those who have it may not realize it, due to a lack of symptoms, it can go untreated for years. Meanwhile, it is potentially damaging the heart, blood vessels, kidneys, and other body parts of those affected.

The good news is that tapping—like yoga, meditation, and other calming practices that focus on keeping your energy flowing properly—helps eliminate high blood pressure by lowering stress levels.

Relationship Issues

Relationship disharmony and conflicts arise regardless of how much in love both parties are. This is a problem for two reasons. First, it's well-known that human beings take out their anxiety and worries on the ones they are closest to—the same ones who are often the least deserving. Second, if one person has a problem, it is not the other's role to fix it. Very simply, this is because you cannot "fix" another person; that person needs to fix him- or herself.

Tapping helps you deal with relationship issues, because the practice helps you attain clarity as well as maintain your own health and stability. With clarity and calm comes the ability to make better decisions.

Allergies

Allergic reactions occur when a person's immune system reacts in a hypersensitive way to normally harmless substances. Allergies can be both hereditary and environmentally based. The most common allergies are environmental: various pollens, smog, foods, bees and other insects, dog hair, cat dander, latex, and the far more life-threatening drug allergies.

The regular practice of tapping helps keep your body functioning at its peak, and this in turn keeps your immune system healthy. If you are allergic to bees, you will always have to carry epinephrine as a precaution, but if you do get stung, your immune system has a far better chance of combating the severity of your reaction.

Fears and Phobias

Fears are, for the most part, completely normal. Fear of snakes, mice, or spiders are all very common. A phobia is a different matter. A phobia is an intense fear of something that in reality poses little or no actual danger. Common phobias include being trapped in closed-in places, heights, and highway driving. Fear is a normal and protective instinct; it activates the automatic fight-or-flight response that has always been crucial to human survival. Phobias do not fall into this category. When normal fear morphs into a phobia, your freedom of reaction is restricted.

Understanding and acknowledging what you are afraid of allows you to begin to overcome a phobia. Tapping can and does help because one of the key affirmations is "I accept."

Addictions

Tapping can indeed help you beat an addiction—to cigarettes, alcohol, caffeine, chocolate, shopping, and more. That's because the underlying cause of addictions often is anxiety. You are not weak. Addictions are not just a bad habit, and lack of willpower is not the reason you haven't been able to break that addiction. More likely, it's that you simply haven't addressed the true reason for your addiction.

Get rid of the root cause—anxiety—with tapping, and that addiction can cease to be an addiction. You'll be back in control and much happier.

Serious Diseases

The practice of tapping has been validated and documented as a healthy noninvasive technique to help overcome a wide range of serious diseases. This is something we will look at in more depth later in this book. Again, tapping is not meant to replace your physician, nor should you view it as such. Major hospitals and teaching facilities worldwide advocate the practice of meditation, the use of acupuncture, and chiropractic medicine as a part of patients' routines.

The practice of regular tapping and its inherent benefits work in conjunction with the medical world in the same way.

Common Benefits of Tapping

You have read briefly about some of the negative issues that tapping addresses and helps remove from your life. What about the everyday pluses that result for people who practice tapping?

Improved health and eradication of pain might well be the first thoughts that come to your mind. But those are only two of the many benefits you will enjoy. The physical effect of positive, free-flowing energy also improves your mental outlook. That naturally improves your emotional outlook. And therefore your entire life, and your perception of everything in it, improves. If this sounds a bit grandiose and tinged with New Age attitudes, read on for an explanation.

You've heard of an endorphin high—that wonderful feeling of pure happiness that we experience after a run or successfully acing an exam. Tapping, when combined with proper deep breathing, also triggers the release of endorphins and raises serotonin levels. It's like having a built-in, completely natural antidepressant on tap—literally.

The premise is really quite simple: by energizing your brain, you create more harmony and better moods; this directly impacts your outlook on the world. The following are a few examples of the physical and mental improvements you'll achieve with tapping.

Improved Attitude

When you aren't stressing out about something, it automatically becomes less intimidating. For dealing with people, this translates into you being less argumentative, which in turn causes others to cease being defensive. Those wonderful things called logic and reasonableness prevail, and calmness becomes the norm. Fewer hassles and fewer arguments equal less stress and a much-improved environment.

An increased sense of calm and inner peace are just two benefits of tapping.

Increased Calmness

When you feel calm, confident, and serene, it is almost impossible to feel anxious, stressed, antagonistic, and anxiety-ridden. Calm is the opposite of anxious; confidence overrules antagonism. When you focus on and develop the positives, the negatives don't have a chance to interfere. The benefits extend to others: when you feel calm, those around you do as well.

Improved Concentration

An improved ability to focus and concentrate is the natural result of allowing your energy to flow freely. Improved concentration means less stress and less anxiety for the simple reason that when you aren't consumed with worry, you are able to concentrate on and understand the matter at hand, thereby addressing it efficiently and adeptly.

Improved Relationships

When you feel good—at peace within yourself and free of stress, pain, fears, and anxiety—all your relationships become far more positive. This is as true for spouses as it is for coworkers; it is as valid for your children as it is for close friends. When you feel good inside, from head to toe, the world becomes a more loving place. Everything and everyone takes on a new and more gentle mien. Comments, attitudes, and behaviors that once drove you up the wall or made you clench your teeth might now generate a raised eyebrow at most. That's all.

Of course you may still get irritated but—and this is a huge *but*—your irritation is not anger. It doesn't chew you up inside, nor does it send you into tears of frustration. Tapping is both a healing and a "chill-out" practice in this regard. It works.

Improved Productivity

Better quality of life is one of the primary benefits that spring from improving your productivity. The less time you spend worrying and fretting about how to accomplish a task, the more time you have to spend doing other things. That new-found extra time can be used purely for your own enjoyment.

A boost in productivity at work makes you shine. When you demonstrate success in your role, new responsibilities, increased pay, and greater job satisfaction are the natural results. Improving your productivity in your personal endeavors—from playing tennis to spending fun time with your kids—means you'll be happier overall.

How do you achieve this? With tapping, you eliminate stress and anxiety, which allows you to gain the ability to concentrate, absorb, and apply and process new information and then make logical, well-thought-out decisions. Concentration and thinking, analytically or creatively, are much easier when stress and anxiety are not present. Getting rid of the negative emotions and fears will boost your productivity a hundredfold, allowing you to make life and everything you do in it more enjoyable.

4

WHAT MAKES TAPPING WORK?

To understand what's involved in tapping and how it works, you first need to understand a little about energy and meridians. Let's take a look at meridians and how they relate to tapping.

In tapping, or EFT (Emotional Freedom Technique), the "discovery statement" is the basic premise for everything that follows:

> It is a disruption within the body's normal energy system and flow that is the source of negative emotions.

Our Bodies Are Comprised of Energy

The human body is made up of electrical energy. That energy is what allows you to feel pain if you burn your hand, cut your finger, or stub your toe. The sensation of pain is electronically and instantly conveyed to your brain; it is the acknowledgment of pain that triggers the innate reaction of pulling your hand back or hopping around yelling, "Ouch!"

These electrical messages are constantly being transmitted to our brains. Our senses respond to things around us all the time. If a flower smells good, you know it without having to look at that flower and go through the process of thinking: "This is a flower. The flower looks like a red rose. Red roses smell nice. Aha, so this red rose smells good." You don't need to see the rose to recognize the scent; the electrical impulses in your body send the aroma directly to your brain and you recognize that it smells good.

If our bodies were not made up of this electrical energy, we would not be able to see, hear, smell, feel, or taste. Medical science makes extensive use of both electroencephalographs (EEGs) to record the electrical activity of the brain and electrocardiographs (EKGs) to record the electrical activity of the heart. The fact that human beings are comprised of electrical energy is a long-documented fact.

So with that knowledge, the questions become, "How do we use this energy to feel better, happier, and more stabilized?" and "How does this energy travel throughout our bodies to our brains?"

Meridians: The Roads by Which Energy Travels

Meridians are, in essence, our electrical circuits; they are the roads by which our energy travels from all parts of our body to our brain. Meridians are what Chinese health practitioners discovered 5,000 years ago, and they form the basis for today's acupuncture, acupressure, massage therapies, and other healing techniques.

It should be noted that a number of indigenous cultures around the world understood this concept of energy traveling through the body and used it as a central basis for healing as well. None of them detailed it as explicitly as the Chinese, however, which is why we most often reference the Asian origins of the concept.

Here's a way to think about the effect of energy flow on your well-being: If you put your T-shirt on backward, it doesn't fit quite right. Your head still goes into the neck and your arms in the sleeves, but the shirt is tight and restrictive. Your arms can't move quite as comfortably as they should; your neck feels as if you have a tie on that is too tight. You can still wear your T-shirt; it just doesn't feel comfortable.

This might seem like a silly example, but when your energy meridians are blocked, the effect is similar. You don't feel your best or 100 percent. Just as the backward T-shirt makes you feel constricted, your body becomes restricted when your natural positive energy can't flow properly throughout your body's meridians to the specific areas of your brain.

Now compare that analogy to one describing proper energy flow between a magnet and your refrigerator door. The magnet should hold your "To Do" list to the refrigerator. If you face the nonmagnetic side to the refrigerator, everything just falls to the floor. You need to align the positive part of the magnet to the negative side of the door to generate energy flow to hold the list up. Turn the magnet around so that it's positioned correctly, and your list stays up; turn your T-shirt around and you're comfortable in your clothes.

Allow your body to function optimally as it should. Open up your internal electrical circuits, and your body will be healthier emotionally and physically.

Meridian Locations

The image in Chapter 1 shows a sample of the human body's meridians and the pathways that energy travels along within your body. Unlike for that biology class from years past, it isn't important to memorize anything here.

What is crucial for you to understand is that the cause of all negative emotions—which affect your physical well-being as much as your mental health and happiness—is a disruption in your body's energy system or circuitry. You've already discovered that a great deal of our physical illnesses have their root cause in the emotions. These negative and unwanted emotions are caused by energy disruptions.

So how do we keep our energy paths, our meridians, open and working properly? This is where tapping comes into play.

Tapping Points and Meridians

The following chapters will walk you through the process of how tapping points relate to and open up your meridians. Included are easy-to-follow graphics so that locating your meridian points and learning to tap couldn't be easier. Tapping has a well-defined and quickly memorized sequence. Basically, you start at the top of your body and work down.

Let's first look at how you can tell if tapping is working for you.

What to Expect with Tapping

Many people experience an improvement after a single round of the tapping sequence. For others, it might take a few sessions. For some people, the initial change can be swift, followed by more gradual improvement; for others, the changes might come incrementally, but consistently showing improvement with each step.

The important thing to remember is that the consistency of your tapping practice *does* matter. In many ways, it is quite similar to chiropractic treatments: Most people visit a chiropractor for the first time when they hurt. The back or neck pain has reached the point of too much pain, and they're scared. Or the sciatic nerve that they never knew was there is loudly telling them it exists—and hurts!

It takes a few (and depending on the extent of the injury and your general physical condition, sometimes more) visits to the chiropractor to get readjusted. Once the spine is realigned properly and stabilized, the visits to the chiropractor become maintenance visits rather than corrective ones.

The practice of tapping has many parallels. There are a few reasons why chiropractic is used as the example:

> Tapping is based on the same core scientific principles as acupuncture, chiropractic, and acupressure—the need for energy to flow freely.

> For all of these practices, the highways for energy are via the meridians.

> In the United States, a greater percentage of people see or have seen a chiropractor rather than an acupuncturist, so the parallel is more easily understood.

Exactly like yoga or meditation, you benefit the most when tapping is done daily. Both yoga and meditation suggest that the practitioner spend a few minutes in the morning and in the evening going through a routine. In fact, a primary routine in yoga is called the "Sun Salutation," and it's designed to awaken and stretch your body after a night's sleep. The evening yoga routine is designed to relax your body and mind after the day. Both routines take less than five minutes, and the benefits are well known. Meditation requires more time—from fifteen to twenty minutes in the morning and again in the evening—but the need to perform it consistently is the same.

Yoga and meditation are similar in intent but still very different in practice. Both rely on deep breathing as an elemental factor in helping clear the mind and body (i.e., your meridians). Yoga is obviously more physical, as stretching is key. Meditation is more directly focused inward. The two practices concentrate on different aspects to achieve similar results.

All three practices—yoga, meditation, and tapping—focus on and greatly improve your health, your peace of mind, and your natural ability to be positive in both attitude and emotion.

Tapping does not stretch your body as yoga does. That is not its intent or purpose. Nor does tapping elevate your mind as meditation does. Again, that is not its intent or purpose. What tapping does do is focus on eliminating the negative energy that is at the root of what is troubling you both mentally and physically. It achieves results in a short space of time. As stated earlier, the timing of results can differ from person to person, but the changes occur within a short time frame for all.

The intent of tapping is to clear energy blockages; this in turn allows your energy to flow uninhibited throughout your body and brain. By creating open passageways for positive energy to flow freely through you, tapping leaves no room for the negative forces that wreak havoc on your body, mind, and heart.

A wonderful old adage states, "Expect nothing. Gain much." As you move into what might be your first experience with tapping, we suggest you adapt it as follows:

> Expect nothing. Be surprised—pleasantly surprised.

Tapping, like yoga or meditation, is best thought of as a practice. To get the most out of tapping, practice it regularly—persistence pays off.

5

THE HOW-TO OF
THE TAPPING PROCESS

Tapping is a physical and mental step-by-step process that works with your body's natural rhythm and pressure points, and it is far easier than it appears upon first reading.

There are two basic segments for each tapping session as delineated by Emotional Freedom Technique (EFT) practitioners:

1. Preparation and affirmation

2. Tapping sequence

Step 1: Preparation and Affirmation

The preparation is when you actually make your body receptive to the positive flowing energy that tapping brings about.

In essence, you are removing the negative and harmful blockages along your meridians so that positive and healing energy can replace them.

During the preparation, you repeat your affirmation three times. Your affirmation acknowledges your concern, fear, or problem, and it creates self-acceptance despite the existence of the issue you are dealing with. (See examples of affirmations for specific issues in the chapters that follow.)

As you repeat your affirmation three times, you will be rubbing a "tender spot" or tapping on your "karate chop" point, both of which are explained in this chapter.

Tender Spots

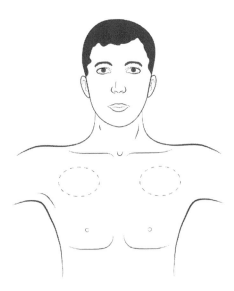

You have two tender spots. To locate them, find the indentation spot at the top of your sternum, or breastbone. That's right where you feel the hollow at the base of your neck. From the curved bottom part of that indentation area, move your finger down about 3 inches toward your belly button and about 3 inches to the left or right. If you exert some pressure in that area, you'll find a tender spot.

When you use a bit of pressure and rub either of these spots, they feel sore or tender because lymphatic congestion occurs there. Rubbing the area disperses the congestion. With a bit of time, the soreness goes away.

Karate Chop Point

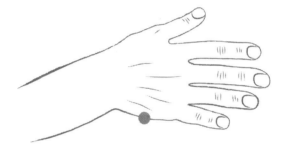

As the name suggests, your karate chop point is on your hand where you would use it in karate. Along the outside of your hand, 1 or 2 inches below the base of your little finger, find the area that has the most flesh—it's the spongy area between the base of your pinky finger and your wrist.

Tap your karate chop point with the tips of your index and middle fingers of the other hand. This is easiest to do if you tap using your dominant hand: If you are right-handed, use your right index and middle fingers to tap on the karate chop point on your left hand. If you are left-handed, use your left index and middle fingers to tap on the karate chop point on your right hand.

Putting It All Together

To complete the preparation and affirmation process, combine the two techniques into one action. Say your affirmation three times while either rubbing a tender spot or tapping your karate chop point. After your first time or two, the preparation and affirmation segment will take perhaps ten seconds. It really is much easier to do than to read about.

Things to know:

> ➤ You do not necessarily have to believe your affirmations.

> ➤ Affirmations are more effective if spoken aloud.

> ➤ Affirmations are more effective if spoken with feeling and sincerity.

The latter two actions are not vital, although they are helpful. Do what is most comfortable for you under the circumstances. You can go through the preparation process anytime and anywhere. There is no reason to be sequestered in a dark room, unless that is what you want. You can go through the preparation in your office with the door wide open or on a park bench—wherever and whenever you feel like it.

Remember, you can use either a tender spot or your karate chop point; this depends on what is most comfortable for you given your specific conditions. You are now ready to proceed to the next step, which is the tapping sequence.

Step 2: Tapping Sequence

This is where all those meridian points you've been reading about come into play. Each designated tapping area (thirteen in total) directly correlates to a primary energy meridian point. Every meridian has two end points. Tap on one end to balance out any disruptions that may exist along the meridian. These end points are near the surface of the body and are readily accessible.

Some people use both hands to tap their meridian points; others just use one hand and the appropriate side of the body. The benefit of using both hands is that you reach a larger area around the meridian point. Using your predominant hand, tap with the flat tips of your index and middle fingers. Tap about seven times in each area that this section describes.

There are three parts of your body where you will be tapping:

> ➤ Head and face

> ➤ Neck and upper body

> ➤ Hands

Some EFT practitioners use letters of the alphabet to denote the specific areas where you will be tapping. This book uses numbers instead, as they are easier to remember. Simply start with Point 1 on the top of your head and work downward through Point 13.

Head and Face Points

On your head and face there are either five or six tapping areas. Some practitioners include the top of the head as is done here, but don't be alarmed if your researched material doesn't always include it.

Point 1: Top of Head

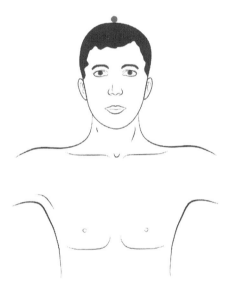

Point 1 is at the top center of your head. This area is easy to find: pretend you are a marionette and the string that makes you stand straight up attaches to the very center of the top of your head. Using both hands, tap 7 times.

Point 2: Eyebrow

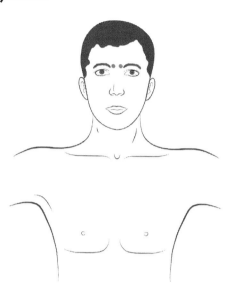

Point 2 is at the inside corners of where your eyebrows begin—just above your nose. Using both hands, tap 7 times.

Point 3: Side of Eye

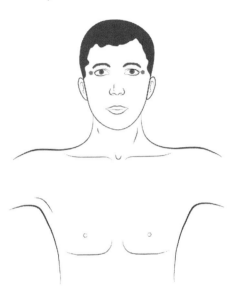

Point 3 is at the outside corners of your eyes, right where those fine lines or crow's-feet appear. Using both hands, tap 7 times.

Point 4: Under Eye

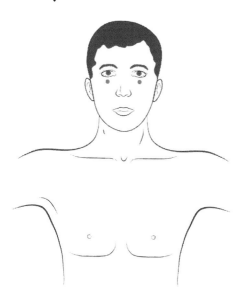

Point 4 is below your eyes. Run your fingers along the upper part of your cheekbones just underneath your eyes. Now find the spots along that bone that are directly below your pupils. They will feel fleshier than other areas along the bone. Using both hands, tap 7 times.

Point 5: Under Nose

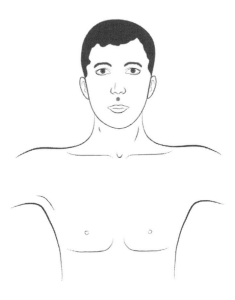

Point 5 is the natural indentation spot between the bottom of your nose and the top of your upper lip. This area is small, and tapping with only one hand is much easier. Tap 7 times.

Point 6: Chin

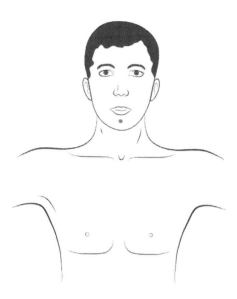

Point 6 is the natural indentation spot midway between the rounded projection of your chin and the bottom of your lower lip. Here as well, one-handed tapping might be easier, as this area is relatively small. Tap 7 times.

Neck and Upper Body Points

There are two tapping areas here. Point 8, the one along your side, can be eliminated if you are tapping in a public setting and feel awkward. Do include it at other times, however.

Point 7: Collarbone

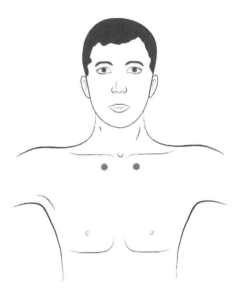

To find Point 7, locate that same curved hollow where your sternum and collarbone meet. From the bottom of this curved indentation, move your fingers down toward your belly button 1 inch or so, and then go to the left and right approximately 1 inch along the collarbone. Using both hands, tap 7 times.

Point 8: Underarm

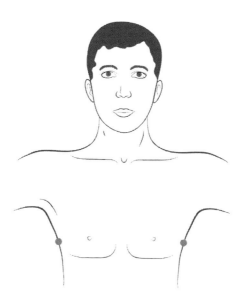

Point 8 is under each arm on your sides in the rib cage area. The easiest way to locate this the first time is to raise one arm and feel around about 4 inches below your armpit. When tapping with both hands, simply repeat Point 8 for each side. Tap 7 times.

Hand Points

You do not need to go through the full routine of tapping each hand unless you elect to do so. Rather, it is easiest to perform the actual tapping with your predominant hand, meaning you will be tapping on your nondominant hand. Right-handed people will tap with their right index and middle fingers on their left hand, and left-handed people will tap with their left index and middle fingers on their right hand.

Point 9: Thumb

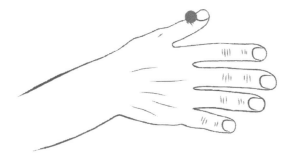

Point 9 is on your thumb. The meridian end is closest to the surface at the outer edge of your thumb at the corner of the fingernail base. Tap 7 times.

Point 10: Index Finger

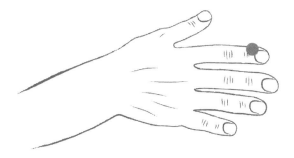

Point 10 is on your index finger. Find the same spot as on your thumb where the corner of the fingernail base meets the outer edge of your index finger (the side facing your thumb). Tap 7 times.

Point 11: Middle Finger

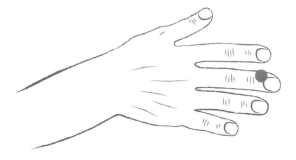

As with Point 10, Point 11 is the spot on your middle finger where the corner of the fingernail base meets the edge of your finger (the side facing your index finger). Tap 7 times.

Point 12: Little Finger

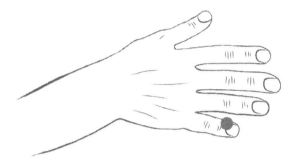

Point 12 is on your little (or pinky) finger. (Note that you are skipping the ring finger.) Once again, you want the spot on your little finger where the corner of the fingernail base meets the inside edge of your finger (facing your ring finger). Tap 7 times.

Point 13: Karate Chop

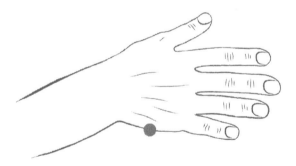

At last you have Point 13, which is the karate chop point. You've already located this point in the preparation and affirmation stage, but just as a reminder, we are including it here. On the outside of your hand there is a fleshy spot between the base of your little finger and your wrist bone. Tap 7 times.

6

USING TAPPING AS AN IMMEDIATE
RESTORATIVE TECHNIQUE

Tapping can be used as an instant restorative or calming technique without spending much time at all. The release of endorphins and the raised serotonin level you experience means that just a few minutes of tapping and deep breathing when you first wake up can make you feel energized. The same brief routine when you're in bed just before going to sleep helps ensure a healthy and restorative night.

Stressed before an exam, an interview, a trip to the dentist, an important presentation, or a client meeting? All you need is a minute or two to become instantly calmer with a vastly improved ability to concentrate and focus.

Deep breathing exercises before, during, or after stressful situations have an almost instant calming effect.

The Quick Version

Combine a tapping routine with deep breathing for at least sixty seconds in any situation, and the results will amaze you. Those sixty seconds quiet your disrupted energy system. You'll feel calmer. You'll be more in control of the way you feel and react.

This abbreviated version of tapping and deep breathing is not sufficient to address serious issues or chronic illnesses. It is, however, very effective as an instant fix or a "calm-me-down" and "de-stressing" technique to unwind and focus.

Note: If deep breathing is difficult for you for any reason such as severe anxiety or a proclivity for panic attacks, do not use the quick version of tapping. Work within the full tapping process until your panic attacks have disappeared.

A short, 60 second tapping session, combined with deep breathing,
can be done almost anywhere and in any situation.

7

TAPPING AWAY EMOTIONAL ISSUES: SUCCESS STORIES

From stresses to teenage angst, from relationship issues to anxiety, the following examples of emotional concerns show how tapping is used to understand and resolve these problems. These success stories can inspire you, including specific tips for applying solutions in your own life. Use the affirmation provided in each category, or modify and apply it to your unique situation.

Stress

Stress is the cause of many problems—physical, mental, and emotional. It certainly ties into, impacts, and intensifies every ailment. Is it the root cause? In many cases, yes. In all cases, it is a proven intensifier for any other issue. The most common definition of stress is that it simply is a reaction to a stimulus that disturbs a person's physical or mental equilibrium. It is the body's way of reacting to a challenge. Stress typically describes a condition that can affect an organism's mental and physical well-being.

Daily life is filled with obligations to be met, routines to be adhered to, and constant and often conflicting time-frame requirements and needs. The baby cries while you're on the phone with a client who thinks you are in the office; the program you were hoping would move you up the corporate ladder just got shelved because the new executive changed gears and didn't tell anyone . . . you've probably experienced it all.

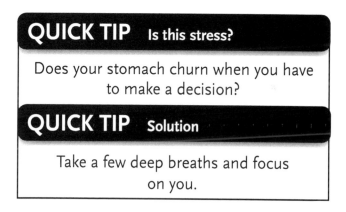

QUICK TIP Is this stress?

Does your stomach churn when you have to make a decision?

QUICK TIP Solution

Take a few deep breaths and focus on you.

Stress is also self-imposed. "Why can't I be the guy who attracts all the women?" "Why aren't I as beautiful and popular as that woman?" "Why can't I afford to send my child to that private school?" "Why aren't I smarter/cooler/richer?" The list is as endless as each person's desires and feelings of insecurity.

Let's be honest: stress will always be a part of life, even if you win the lottery. Learning to divert and master stress is the crucial element to keeping it from overrunning your life. Tapping is a natural doorway into mitigating the adverse effects of stress, as the full tapping process releases the negative blockages and allows your energy to flow fully and freely.

The following affirmation can be used to handle stress:

affirmation

Even though I feel
overwhelmingly stressed,
I deeply and completely
recognize and accept
myself.

Your words of affirmation allow you to acknowledge the problem and accept yourself in spite of it.

Summarized Case Study 7-1: Career Stress

Not all stress comes from within, but we do internalize and react to other people's stress—making it ours!

A friend of mine was under immense pressure at work; she is an upper-level executive in a highly competitive industry, and her boss wants everything yesterday. Like many of us, she is also doing the perennial balancing act between family and work, and far too often she feels like her family gets the short end of the deal—and of her. A career she loved has turned into an all-consuming nightmare.

As we talked about how she could deal with the issue and come out ahead of the game, it became apparent that her boss was a micromanager, but her role needed flexibility to be done properly. His management style simply prohibited her from performing as needed.

As I lead her through a series of tapping exercises, we addressed not only what she was feeling but why the situation existed in the first place. She quickly discovered that her boss was insecure—hence the micromanaging.

With the realization of the cause, she was able to formulate a way to help him feel more secure in his role and to restore her pleasure in work.

Anxiety

Anxiety is a mood—an unpleasant state of inner turmoil. It's often accompanied by nervous behavior, fatigue, muscular tension, and difficulty sleeping. This general feeling of anxiety, unpleasant as it is, is far different from what we term "anxiety disorders" and should not be confused with the latter.

Stress and anxiety often go hand in hand, as stress leads to pervasive anxiety in many instances. Anxiety can be as temporary as quaking knees and a dry mouth before giving a public speech, or it can present itself as overwhelming feelings of anxiety about almost everything in your life. Financial concerns are one of the most common causes for anxiety; job insecurity is another.

If you're a parent, you've probably felt anxiety about a child. Usually this is normal, but not so all the time. If your anxiety for the child is overprotective, you can do harm to the child's normal development and ability to acquire social skills.

It is important to recognize when anxiety is short term and normal, and when anxiety can become problematic. If you suffer from inexplicable anxiety, tapping can help you overcome it. Anxiety, like stress, causes the body's natural flow of energy to misfire—to form blockages along the meridian points. This can lead to more severe issues. By taking preventive measures to manage anxiety before it takes over, you will be much more equipped to keep it in check permanently.

This affirmation can be used to handle anxiety:

affirmation

Even though I feel
overwhelming anxiety,
I deeply and completely
recognize and accept
myself.

Your words of affirmation allow you to acknowledge the problem and accept yourself in spite of it.

Social anxiety can run the gamut from debilitating shyness to an inability to do one's job; it has no age boundaries and the results can range from awkward to disastrous. Given the vastly diverse causes for anxiety, the following two very common examples demonstrate how the tapping process can help make your life far more pleasurable.

QUICK TIP Is this anxiety?

Does the thought of walking into a room full of strangers turn you into a quivering jellyfish?

QUICK TIP Solution

Focus on one or two individuals. This makes the situation less intimidating.

Summarized Case Study 7-2: Social Anxiety

Anxiety, specifically social anxiety, impacts virtually every aspect of a person's life.

Social anxiety might appear to be a severe case of shyness, but when it makes a person chronically terrified to deal with groups of people, it becomes more than shyness.

Eddie was one such person: he was a wonderful and prolific writer, but when it came time to promote his books, he simply couldn't handle the social interaction. Even though he understood and accepted that writers needed to promote their work to be successful, Eddie became stiff with fear when he had to speak publicly at book-signing events. He had to stand in front of the attendees, read an excerpt, and hold a question-and-answer session afterward. He dreaded it every time. His concentration wavered and he dripped with perspiration, which only exacerbated his anxiety. The more press tours the publisher would set up, the more Eddie considered ditching his career.

Luckily, Eddie's publisher practiced tapping. When he finally discovered why his recalcitrant author was so resistant to doing any more tours, he shared the concept and suggested Eddie try it. He set Eddie up with an EFT practitioner, and after one tapping session, Eddie was a committed advocate.

Today, Eddie still writes books and actually enjoys meeting his adoring public.

QUICK TIP   Is this anxiety?

Do you dread the thought of getting on a plane, or even going to an airport?

QUICK TIP   Solution

Write out an affirmation to address your fear of flying. Don't worry about the "why"—that will come.

Summarized Case Study 7-3: Fear of Flying

Fear of flying is a fairly common concern, and it's one that severely restricts a person's sense of adventure!

Flight anxiety can be due to a number of issues, ranging from claustrophobia, to fear of heights, to not being in the proverbial driver's seat (i.e., relinquishing control of your life). Being terrified to board a plane can restrict upward career mobility, and it certainly takes the fun out of a holiday.

Susan was one of these people. A friend told her about tapping, she learned the techniques, and it helped put an end to her phobic fear. Today she travels all the time by plane.

Teenage Angst

First, if you're a parent of a teenager, you truly need to remember what your teenage years were like. Selective memory may have turned them into a completely joyous, carefree time in your mind, but the teen years are tough for more reasons than were previously thought. The mood swings, insecurities, and rebellions are due to more than just raging hormones.

The teenage brain is in developmental flux. To be exact, the frontal cortex of the brain is still developing, and the ability to reason and form logical judgments resides in the frontal cortex. In other words, the teenage brain does not have a complete and mature neural structure in place.

Adolescents cannot think things through like adults can. In fact, reasoning and judgment continue to develop well into the twenties. Teens may be physically mature from a biological standpoint, but they are not emotionally mature, nor should that be expected of them. There is far more truth to the line "you look like an adult, but you act like a toddler" than we ever realized.

Along with this brain immaturity are the hormonal changes that accompany adolescence. The barrage of challenges teens have to face during these years are emotional, physical, and academic. To say the teenage years are extremely stressful is putting it mildly.

Some causes of teenage stress include:

- Hormones and bodily changes, which can lead to emotional outbursts, weight gain, acne, and more

- Poor body image

- Constantly feeling vulnerable

- Feeling like a misfit or unable to measure up to others, which causes low self-esteem

- Academic stress and test-taking anxiety

- Home life disruptions, such as moving or changing schools

- Bullying, fear of being bullied, or pressure to be a bully

- Pressures related to career choices

- Conflict with parents, teachers, siblings, and friends

- Peer pressure to experiment with alcohol, sex, or drugs

- Financial pressure in keeping up with fashion trends

- Taking on too much and not getting enough sleep

- Possibly trauma or the death of a family member or friend

- Above all, trying to define who they really are

No wonder teenagers feel overwhelmed, anxious, vulnerable, and alone. And it is no wonder you view the teenager in your home as volatile.

Have you noticed a key word throughout this discussion? It's *stress*. By now you have a firm understanding of the havoc that stress and anxiety can wreak on one's emotional and physical well-being. You also have knowledge of some coping tools that can help. You are in a perfect position to share the tapping practice and process with your teen so he or she might benefit as well. You can also reach out to EFT practitioners, if that is more comfortable. In doing so, you will be giving your kids a tool that will last a lifetime—and make those teenage years far more enjoyable for the entire family.

Teens don't need to know the theory behind tapping. They just want to be better, happier, and healthier. Once they know the tool helps them achieve this, they might ask you how it works and why.

The following affirmation can be used by tweens and teens to handle day-to-day living:

affirmation

Even though I have this overwhelming fear, I deeply and completely recognize and accept myself.

These words of affirmation allow your teen to acknowledge the problem and accept him- or herself in spite of it.

Summarized Case Study 7-4: Teenage Turmoil

Living with a teenager can be like living with Dr. Jekyll and Mr. Hyde . . .

Lisa and her teenage daughter had a conversation that went along these lines:

DAUGHTER: You don't get it! You don't have a clue how I feel!

LISA: Sweetie, I do get it. You want to go away for the weekend with your friends. You want to camp out on the beach and surf. I understand camping out and surfing. I did those things. What I will not permit is your going without an adult in the crowd.

DAUGHTER: I'm not you! It's different! What are you thinking? That I'm dumb enough to do drugs or something? Why don't you trust me?

LISA: Of course not. I do trust you, and I know and like all your friends. I really do trust you. But I don't trust some lunatic who might stumble across half a dozen teenage girls camping on a beach. You may not go without an adult.

DAUGHTER: I HATE you!

Sound familiar? You can change the details of the scenario, but the crux of the message stays the same. To a teenager, parents simply don't get it! Slam. Bang.

Lisa's daughter practices tapping—she became interested because she was curious about it.

Sometime between her final angry outburst and when she emerged from her room thirty minutes later, Lisa's daughter had gone through her tapping routine and was noticeably more relaxed.

DAUGHTER: Mom, do you think Uncle Dave would like to haul out his surfboard this weekend and go with us?

While tapping won't stop your teenagers from having emotional outbursts and experiencing inner turmoil, it will offer them a chance to calm down and collect their thoughts in a rational way so battles aren't drawn out and compromises can be made. Their stresses will be minimized, and they will be much more pleasant company.

QUICK TIP   Teen behaving badly?

This is totally normal!
While not always easy to live with,
it's part of growing up.

QUICK TIP   Solution

Introduce your teenager
to tapping, even if you don't
practice it yourself.

Relationship Issues

Relationships fall into multiple categories: spouse or partner, kids, extended family, friends, peers, and coworkers,
employees, or bosses. Different negative emotions arise in
all relationships, and there is no one-cure-fits-all solution.

What is most important to understand is that if you can
transform the negative emotions you feel in any one situation into something inconsequential, you will be much better
off. Your stress level dissipates, anxiety is reduced, and with
that 99 percent of the problem disappears. The issue is not
necessarily solved, but you are far more able to be objective
about the situation and then resolve or diffuse it.

Let's put this into perspective with a few examples.

Work: A relationship at work is causing you stress, angst,
and escalating anger. You like your job (and the paycheck),
but so-and-so is such an idiot, you are ready to pitch a fit and
quit in frustration.

Children: No, you cannot (nor do you really want to) divorce your
child, but there are days when you are ready to do exactly that.

Partner: Our partners get the worst of all our stress and negative emotions because they are a safe haven where we can
"let it all out." What we often forget as we rant about things
that bother us is that the listener might need to rant as well,
but doesn't because you are. This doesn't mean you shouldn't
discuss things with them, but it does mean you shouldn't

inundate your partner with negative emotions—whether they are the cause or not. That doesn't work, and it certainly doesn't change the actions, behaviors, or words that upset you.

> ## QUICK TIP   Loved one drifting away?
>
> It is not the "seven-year itch"—it's because your relationship is mired in everyday life and stress.
>
> ## QUICK TIP   Solution
>
> Actively affirm that your relationship is solid; then address the areas for improvement.

Tapping allows you to get rid of those negative, conflicting, and restrictive emotions so you can see things with more clarity and put it all into perspective. Honestly, half the time you'll laugh at yourself for getting so upset earlier. By performing a tapping routine, you will feel significantly better all the time—emotionally, mentally, and physically—which helps you maintain your own health and stability. Your relationships will be more harmonious and beneficial for both parties as a result.

There are almost certainly hidden or underlying reasons for your reactions of frustration, anger, impatience, and so on—all of those negative feelings impact and can endanger relationships. The practice and process of regular tapping will help you acknowledge and address the root cause, but the immediate effect (which is what you need in the moment) will be to give you peace of mind and calmness.

The following affirmation can be used to handle relationship issues:

affirmation

Even though I have this overwhelming desire to leave you, I deeply and completely recognize and accept myself.

Summarized Case Study 7-5: Relationship Issues

Relationships are tough. For some it is harder to trust than for others, but no relationship will be endless hand-holding and kisses.

This chapter has already covered kids, friends, family, and work relationships, so this example focuses on the relationship between partners. Always remember that all issues, causes, and solutions are applicable to many situations and titles.

For this case study, let's look at a first-person account from Susan:

I've been married long enough to have a teenager and a pre-teen. We didn't marry until a few years after college and didn't have kids for a few years after that. I was no starry-eyed kid, rather a professional woman with a career and a full life.

Not too long ago, I felt as if my husband and I were drifting apart. I could not put my finger on anything specific—no single instance. I couldn't even figure out where to cast the blame. It wasn't a normal marital tiff. We'd had enough of those over the years for me to know one when I experienced it.

I loved my husband, but I was feeling blah in capital letters: BLAH. I also knew I had to resolve whatever was going on—that is, why I felt that way.

My confusion and fear were partially troublesome because my "cure" for so much had been my practice of tapping. If my energy was all flowing smoothly and openly, why wasn't I feeling the positive energy and optimism that tapping brings?

I decided to have a weekend away just for me. I needed to be alone to discover what was going on. I headed to one of my favorite small beach towns miles from anywhere. I could walk the beach in solitude, play in the surf, and build sand castles while I tried to figure out what was going on and how to correct it.

That weekend I must have gone through the tapping process more times than many people do in years. What I discovered shocked me. A memory I had absolutely no recollection of suddenly surfaced. I couldn't have been more than a few years old, but suddenly that event was crystal clear.

By uncovering this memory via an open mind and body, and acknowledging its impact on my feelings of dissatisfaction and unhappiness, I was able to address and resolve that negativity that had been plaguing my marriage. This allowed me and my husband to move forward with free communication, renewed closeness, and deeper understanding.

Depression

Depression is not just a passing sadness or a period of feeling down—it affects the ability to function normally and find enjoyment in life. It can lead to academic, social, economic, and also physical problems. One of the most common results of depression is failed relationships with friends, family, and loved ones. Severe depression can lead to catastrophic health failures and to suicide.

Because medical science has tended to treat depression as a chemical imbalance rather than as an electrical energy circuit blockage or misfire, drugs are the most common treatment. The greatest concern with medications is that they do not solve the problem. Prescription medication simply covers up the core cause.

Pills are an easy-to-swallow combination of compressed chemicals. By introducing a foreign substance or combination of foreign substances into your body, the result invariably includes side effects. All chemicals cause side effects. That is the primary reason why when you are prescribed one medication, your doctor monitors you closely and very often prescribes other medications to temper your body's reaction in areas that are not being treated. The end result: you ingest more chemicals that throw off your body's normal and healthy cycles and rhythm. Frankly, this is a self-defeating pattern.

Tapping has been shown to address the base reasons for depression without the need for chemicals or medications. The practice of tapping allows the healthy restoration of the electrical energy circuit to the brain, and your body takes over from there. Depression—like stress, anxiety, and the plethora of other issues we address in this book—can be the result of negative emotions.

Recall the discovery statement that serves as the basic premise for tapping:

> It is a disruption within the body's normal energy system and flow that is the source of negative emotions.

Approaching and dealing with depression under this guidance can and does eliminate it. By using tapping to allow for free positive energy flow, you will be well on the way to understanding and resolving depression.

The following affirmation can be used to handle depression:

affirmation

Even though I feel
overwhelming despair, I deeply
and completely recognize and
accept myself.

Summarized Case Study 7-6: Depression

The root cause of depression might be unwarranted (and unrec-ognized) guilt.

Depression, as you have learned, can come from multiple sources and often springs from unacknowledged events, such as a traumatic loss or long-submerged childhood memories. You may experience symptoms such as feeling omnipresent fatigue or hopelessness, or even just a general apathy in your life.

Jane's son was dealing with severe depression over his roommate's death in a car accident. Her son was not in the car during the accident, because he had to study for an exam. He had passed on going out with his pals that night. What he was dealing with was not only the loss of his close friend, but also an incredible, overwhelming feeling of guilt for being alive. He "should" have been in that car, too.

Jane's family preferred to find a drug-free solution for his depression and discovered that tapping not only helped him deal with and accept his roommate's death, but also helped him understand that there was no reason for him to feel responsible. Sad, yes. Guilty, no.

As you continue through this book, remember that any number of events and emotions can cause depression. Negative feelings, if left to their own devices as unaddressed and unresolved issues, can grow into depression. The practice of tapping attempts to hinder the development of depression by keeping that positive energy flowing.

QUICK TIP   Is this depression?

If you have suffered the loss of someone important to you, what you feel could be depression.

QUICK TIP   Solution

Approach your grief and deal with it first. Underlying issues will surface and be healed in the process.

8

TAPPING AWAY PHYSICAL ISSUES:
SUCCESS STORIES

From high blood pressure to weight management, from addiction to countless aches and ailments—the following examples of physical concerns show how tapping is used to understand and resolve these problems. These success stories can inspire you, including specific tips for applying solutions in your own life. Use the affirmation provided in each category, or modify and apply it to your unique situation.

Weight Management

It's no secret: Obesity is a national problem, and it's becoming an international one as well. Our health is predicated on what we eat. Improper diets, lack of exercise, junk food, and poor self-image based on what people have been taught to consider ideal are all part of the problem. There is simply no way a person can claim ignorance.

What falls under the category of weight management? Obesity and anorexia are the extreme ends of the spectrum; in the middle lie issues such as yo-yoing weight, binge eating, and overeating. These are all centered in emotional habits or individual reactions to stressful or unhappy situations.

> ## QUICK TIP Unhealthy eating habits?
>
> Have you ever said something to the effect of: "I really don't eat that much but..."?
>
> ## QUICK TIP Solution
>
> Weight problems are complex. Find the cause, and weight management becomes much easier.

Lack of weight management can lead to the onset of diabetes, heart problems, and any number of emotional and psychological issues. Psychological issues resulting from lack of weight management can run the gamut from anxiety to phobias about appearing in public to destructive addictions because a person is unhappy with his or her self-image and life.

Any number of mothers try to explain away their youngster's excess pounds with "But he/she doesn't eat that much," and "It's baby fat; it will disappear as he/she grows taller." One has to wonder how many of these mothers have looked in their kitchen cabinets lately or whether they really pay attention to what their kids eat.

Eating disorders are, in essence, addictions to a habit. Addictions are caused by various forms of anxiety. Like so much of what is addressed in this book, these disorders are centered around an emotional issue. Dealing with that emotional problem through tapping is a proven path to healthy weight loss, maintenance of a proper weight, and a long-term healthy diet regimen.

The following affirmation can be used to handle weight management:

affirmation

Even though I have this overwhelming desire to eat too much, I deeply and completely recognize and accept myself.

Summarized Case Study 8-1: Weight Gain

Eating disorders involve more than straight caloric intake.

Fad diets are not a long-term solution, as anyone who has tried one knows. *Why* you eat or don't eat is at the base of weight management.

Karen was bemoaning the fact she had put on approximately 20 pounds over the last six months. She was frustrated and embarrassed that she couldn't get back to the weight she wanted to be at. She revealed that her husband had been laid off and the family was dealing with all sorts of stress and worry as a result. An acquaintance brought up the possibility of tapping as a tool to help deal with not just her eating issues, but also the stress and anxiety in her life. The fact that she could do it herself—and for free—was a huge plus and she eagerly agreed to try it.

A few short months later, she was a completely different woman—a more slender, happier, and healthier woman. She used tapping to rid herself of the stress and negative self-esteem, freeing her up to focus on positive energy and productive results.

Diabetes

Diabetes is one of the major medical issues that can result from a history of weight management problems. Diabetes, both type 1 and type 2, affects how your body uses blood glucose. Type 2 diabetes (including prediabetes and gestational diabetes) is the more common of the two; it is often preventable and is reversible to a good extent.

To understand the correlation between weight and diabetes, it is necessary to understand the basics of how our bodies function. Glucose is a main source of energy for the cells that make up muscles and tissues, and glucose is the brain's main source of fuel. Diabetes means you have too much glucose in your blood. Too much glucose can lead to serious health problems.

In a normal, healthy body, the balance between insulin and blood glucose is self-regulating. The pancreas secretes the insulin hormone into the bloodstream. The insulin circulates throughout the bloodstream and enables sugar to enter the cells. This process allows the insulin to lower the amount of sugar in the bloodstream. As the blood sugar level drops, so does the secretion of insulin from the pancreas.

Glucose comes from two primary sources: food intake and the liver. The liver stores and makes glucose. When insulin levels are low, the liver metabolizes the stored glycogen into glucose to keep the glucose level within normal ranges.

> ## QUICK TIP   Do I have diabetes?
>
> "I'm older, I have high blood pressure, and my doctor says I'm at a high risk for diabetes."
>
> ## QUICK TIP   Solution
>
> It's important to maintain a healthy weight and proper blood pressure. Start paying attention to yours now!

In people determined to be prediabetic (pre–type 2) or as having type 2 diabetes, the cells become resistant to the action of insulin, and the pancreas cannot make enough insulin to overcome this resistance. (For type 1 diabetes, the immune system is also involved, but the details are too extensive to elaborate here. Those with type 1 diabetes understand the cause and how to treat it; everyone else needs to understand what can cause type 2 diabetes.)

Type 2 diabetes results in sugar building up in the bloodstream rather than moving into the cells where it's needed for energy. Being overweight is strongly linked to the development of type 2 diabetes, but be aware that not everyone with type 2 diabetes is overweight.

The following are three guiding principles for controlling both types of diabetes:

- ➢ Eat healthy foods.

- ➢ Exercise regularly.

- ➢ Lose excess weight.

Tapping can help you address and resolve diabetes because of the following:

- ➢ Tapping addresses the underlying reasons why you have an eating issue that has led to developing diabetes.

- ➢ Tapping helps keep all your energy systems unblocked and functioning properly.

The following affirmation can be used to cope with diabetes:

affirmation

Even though I have
diabetes (or pre-diabetes),
I deeply and completely
recognize and
accept myself.

Summarized Case Study 8-2: Diabetes Diagnosis

Being diagnosed with diabetes does not mean you can't have fun.

Ken was a dentist who was diagnosed with type 2 diabetes. All his doctor had told him was to lose a few pounds, continue exercising (he played either tennis or racquetball almost daily), eat properly, and try to get his blood pressure down. He wasn't satisfied that those solutions were enough.

His internist gave him a one-month trial period by writing him a very low-dosage prescription, but only with the promise of a follow-up visit one month later. Ken was a 60-year-old man: you might think he wouldn't be quite so surprised or offended by the diagnosis, but not so. He was furious.

On the tennis courts, he regularly beat the pants off players half his age and never even breathes hard. But at 60 years old, some small bits and pieces of his body were possibly wearing out. That's what age does to us.

As Ken explained his situation to a patient one day, she suggested he do some research on what tapping was all about and give it a try. Six months later, Ken was praising the results he achieved with tapping: he no longer had signs of early diabetes and his blood pressure had improved.

High Blood Pressure

High blood pressure is a serious condition that can lead to coronary heart disease, heart failure, stroke, kidney failure, and other health problems. The National Heart, Lung, and Blood Institute estimates that one-third of all adults in the United States suffer from high blood pressure.

In layman's terms, blood pressure is the force of blood pushing against the walls of the arteries as the heart pumps blood. The consequences of high blood pressure? If it rises and stays elevated over time, it can damage the body in many ways. Blood pressure tends to go up with age; there really are no signs or warnings of an impending problem. That's why every visit to the doctor entails the nurse taking your blood pressure. Your doctor is watching for both a trend and any issues.

High blood pressure is caused by a combination of many things and can be mitigated by certain actions. Even though the following rules are common sense, it never hurts to be reminded:

- Avoid excess salt when cooking at home or eating out.

- Stop drinking sodas, as the sodium levels are high.

- Avoid fast food for the same reason.

- Learn to read labels. Canned goods, even those marked "low" or "reduced" sodium, contain more salt than you need. Salt is both a preservative and a flavor enhancer.

- Fresh is best; frozen (without sauces) is next; canned and packaged goods are best avoided.

- Salads are healthy; salad dressings are not. So ditch the bottled dressings. Use fresh lemon juice or olive oil and vinegar.

- Watch your alcohol consumption.

- Don't smoke (see information on addiction in this chapter for more tips).

- Maintain a healthy weight (see information on weight management in this chapter for more tips).

- Exercise on a regular basis.

- Eat healthy: fruits, vegetables, nuts, healthy grains, and proteins. If you eat red meat, do so in small amounts and infrequently.

- De-stress!

QUICK TIP   Have high blood pressure?

Your job is very stressful, and now your doctor tells you that you have high blood pressure.

QUICK TIP   Solution

High blood pressure is often due to a combination of several factors. Find and work to resolve the underlying causes.

Let's talk about that last one: stress. Stress, as you know, is very similar to anxiety. Both are emotionally based in that your mind and body react to external forces and cause an internal reaction. Stress can make your stomach churn, make you short-tempered, impact your ability to sleep properly, and much more.

Using techniques to help alleviate your internalized reactions to and holding of stress will significantly impact your blood pressure levels and other physical side effects. Because the acupressure aspect of tapping opens up all your meridians by removing blockages, it allows proper flow of energy throughout your body and to your brain. When your natural energy flows properly, your body is naturally healthier. Combine that with yoga, meditation, or deep breathing, and you have an all-purpose stress buster that will eradicate the accompanying physical ailments.

The following affirmation can be used to deal with high blood pressure:

affirmation

Even though I have
high blood pressure,
I deeply and completely
recognize and
accept myself.

Summarized Case Study 8-3: High Blood Pressure

Being told you are at risk for serious health consequences is a warning, not a death warrant.

High blood pressure is such a common occurrence that the term doesn't seem to scare us until the doctor, solemn-faced, adds the words *heart attack.*

Paul was in his late forties and a successful entrepreneur with a flourishing business plus interest in a few others. He was active in his community and had a couple of kids in college. He loved art and converted a shed in his backyard into a studio where he painted when he had the time. From all appearances, Paul should be the envy of many. He seemed to have life figured out and to be his own happy person.

One day, seemingly out of the blue, his doctor told him he was a leading candidate for a stroke or a heart attack. His blood pressure was off the charts, and he needed to change his life right away. Neither was Paul overweight nor did he smoke. He was a laid-back guy—that is, he didn't have a hyper personality by any means. And he got regular exercise. So why was his blood pressure out of control?

Paul shared his concern and disbelief with a neighbor while they were walking their dogs. He just couldn't figure out what to do. The next time they ran into each other, Paul's neighbor gave him some basic tapping information and a few website URLs so he could research the method. Paul read everything through. The information made enough sense to him that he did some more investigating on his own and decided to give tapping a try. He changed some other things in his life as well, but he credited the incorporation of tapping into his daily routine as a major positive step in the right direction. His blood pressure improved greatly as a result.

Addiction

Tapping can help you beat that addiction—to cigarettes, alcohol, caffeine, chocolate, shopping, and more. This is because the real cause of addictions is anxiety, not your weakness. Addictions are not a bad habit; lack of willpower is not why you haven't been able to break that addiction. You simply haven't addressed the true reason for your addiction.

It goes without saying that certain highly addictive substances—cigarettes, for example—contain chemicals known to enhance dependency.

QUICK TIP   Feeling hooked?

You can't stop thinking about your next cigarette, drink, or pill. It's not the end of the world: you can turn it around.

QUICK TIP   Solution

Find the real cause: the solution becomes far less intimidating and far more doable.

There is a growing crisis within First-World countries: large segments of the population are becoming addicted to medications. This is also a type of chemical dependency. Earlier chapters discussed how Western medicine is centered on chemical treatments versus nonchemical or holistic cures in other cultures. In many ways this alarming trend is due to erroneous thinking. We cannot fix all our aches and ailments with a pill. That thinking is counterintuitive to the way our bodies were designed to work. It is widely acknowledged that addictions often spring from emotional causes. But addiction is included in this chapter on physical issues because addictions are predicated on foreign substances being ingested.

Approaching the "cure" for your addiction needs to be done on the grounds of why you crave something, not on what you can ingest to counter it.

The following affirmation can be used to handle addiction or dependency issues:

affirmation

Even though I have an
addiction, I deeply and
completely recognize and
accept myself.

Thoughts on Addictions

Addictions are scary to the person dealing with dependence and to everyone who cares about that person.

Alcoholics Anonymous (AA) is the oldest and most established support system for dealing with alcohol addiction. AA (and many other twelve-step programs) begins each meeting with the Serenity Prayer:

God grant me the serenity to accept the things I cannot change,
Courage to change the things I can,
And wisdom to know the difference.

(Niebuhr, n.d.)

The Serenity Prayer is, in many ways, an affirmation that serenity is an absence of anxiety and guilt. You've learned that addiction, deep down, stems from anxiety.

The practice of daily tapping can be used independently or in conjunction with twelve-step programs to help turn your life around. Tapping is a highly effective tool, but you have to want to make use of that tool.

It is important to remember that once you have broken an addiction, it does not mean you will never become re-addicted. You should practice complete abstinence and embrace the attitude of "I will never touch what I was addicted to again. I am forever free *if* I keep myself free."

Not all addictions are as deeply intertwined with our physical makeup as alcohol and drug addictions are, because these are chemically induced.

Some people are addicted to caffeine, be it in the form of coffee, sodas, or tea; others are addicted to chocolate or shopping. Although the chemical components of alcohol and drugs require other interventions to fully eliminate those addictions, dependence on caffeine, food, shopping, and the like can be addressed and eliminated through tapping.

Physical Pain and Other Health Concerns

The practice of tapping has been used to address a wide variety of health problems primarily because negative emotions have intervened with normal body functioning. Meridians get blocked and the body's correct energy flow is interrupted. If you have visited a chiropractor, you've heard the phrase "out of alignment." In acupuncture, acupressure, and tapping, the same "out of alignment" applies, but in relation to energy flow rather than a spine.

It is crucial to remember that most of the time you get sick and your body gets out of whack because negative emotions adversely affect your well-being. Often we do not know the underlying cause, so using an affirmation that acknowledges the pain and accepts it will often begin the healing process. Uncovering and resolving the actual cause usually comes with time.

The following affirmation can be used to handle health issues:

affirmation

Even though I have this overwhelming neck and shoulder pain, I deeply and completely recognize and accept myself.

Tapping can be incorporated into your medical plan and regimen. Tell your physician that you want to or have begun the practice of tapping as an additional tool to deal with your health concerns. Many medical specialists understand the practice, and the numbers are increasing on a regular basis. Work with your doctor to track your progress. Remember, both of you are approaching the same issue from a different perspective. Your doctor reads the charts, blood counts, facts, and figures, but only you can describe how you truly feel and relay that most vital information.

9

FREQUENTLY ASKED QUESTIONS

What follows are your questions and some facts: some subjects are lighthearted and fun, others far more serious. All are honest, common questions; if you have them, so do others.

Q: Should I tell my medical doctor or therapist that I'm trying tapping?

A: Absolutely! Many doctors, therapists, and counselors are aware of the practice of tapping, and that number is only growing. Your physician or therapist may even be a practitioner—it never hurts to ask.

Over the last few years, military personnel returning home have caused a subsequent increase in diagnosed cases of post-traumatic stress disorder (PTSD). As a result, tapping has been incorporated into numerous medical treatments to counter and negate the causes of PTSD. Tapping has been shown to have a profound curative effect on veterans and has helped them move forward with their lives.

It is never pleasant when others have to experience pain and suffering in order for new techniques to be accepted, but unfortunately that has long been the case. Tapping is no different. Crises bring about awareness and innovation. In the case of PTSD, the innovative "cure" had been around for decades, but it took an unprecedented number of confirmed diagnoses to allow Emotional Freedom Technique (EFT) to emerge into accepted usage.

Incorporating tapping into your daily routine, whether for medical purposes or not, is completely holistic. Remember, you are not introducing any foreign substance into your system, nor are you eating according to the latest fad diet. Because tapping relies completely on natural and healthy adjustments of your mind and body, no negative side effects or reactions are possible.

Q: Can I stop taking my medication and use tapping to relieve symptoms associated with my illness?

A: Never stop taking medications or alter the dosage without medical supervision. Complications or side effects may occur, making it potentially dangerous. Many times patients need to be weaned off of medications gradually—not because the medications are addictive, but because the body is used to the drug and relies on it in some way to function "correctly." Helping the body prepare and adapt to being without a drug can take time. The process is different for every individual.

Your physician should work with you to determine a plan that allows you to tap with the intent of healing. Your medications—why they are needed and what for, how they interact with other things you ingest, and so on—should all be discussed in detail, and your progress should be monitored on a regular basis. If you show improvement, your doctor should be willing to ease you off prescribed medications over time as you make progress in helping your body heal.

Q: Is tapping based on religion?

A: No. Religion and religious beliefs are totally unrelated to tapping. The practice is based on 5,000-year-old Chinese acupuncture methods and the Chinese understanding of meridians as the conduits, or internal roads, that our energy travels along from points on our bodies to the receptive areas of our brains.

Meditation, although sometimes tied to Hinduism and other religions, does not relate directly to specific beliefs either. In a similar vein, acupuncture, though developed in a predominantly Buddhist and Taoist country, does not in any way require practitioners to follow either religion.

Q: What if I don't really believe in energy meridians?

A: If the word *meridians* sounds a bit too esoteric for your taste, simply rename *meridian* as *pathway* or *road*. Your internal electrical energy has to travel somehow—and along something—to reach your brain.

As you learned earlier, without meridians (or whatever word you prefer) transporting energy to our brains, we would have none of our five senses. We would not recognize pain or lack of pain. In effect, without our senses and our brain recognizing each sensation for what it is, we would not survive as a species. Our entire bodies make use of electrical activity and energy to transmit information. The word *meridian* is simply a way of explaining that activity.

Q: What does it mean when people say their "energy meridians are blocked"?

A: Blocked energy meridians (or roads) simply mean that your energy isn't flowing as it should for optimum health and happiness. In a way, a blocked meridian can be compared to a blocked or clogged artery. When cholesterol causes a blockage in your arteries, surgery is used to remove the blockage. Unblocking your meridians is much easier and totally noninvasive. No drugs are required; no surgery is required. No recovery time is required; no physical therapy is required. Plus it's free and there's no pain involved—that's the icing on the proverbial cake.

Q: What are the causes of a meridian becoming "blocked"?

A: Meridians become blocked due to negative emotions. Negative emotions, such as stress and anxiety, often lie at the root of more serious concerns, from depression to panic attacks to physical illness in multiple forms.

Negative or destructive emotions wreak havoc with any or all of your emotional, physical, and mental states. Your natural immune system is overtaxed trying to deal with this and responds by not being able to cope as it should. It gets overloaded. It really is no different than when you sometimes feel like screaming or crying in frustration over something out of your control. You want to throw your arms up in the air and yell, "I'm done with this!" You're tired of trying to cope with too much and never making progress.

Tapping allows you to clear out the negative feelings so that only the positive ones remain. When you feel good, everything improves. Your energy returns to its optimal level, and you are healthier and happier in life. When you incorporate tapping into your daily routine, you clear the debris (or the traffic jams) off your internal roads so your energy can travel at the speed it was designed to.

Q: How many tapping sequences do I need to perform before I will start feeling positive results?

A: There really is no right or wrong response to this question. There is no definitive timeline, simply because every single one of us is different. We react differently to any number of things. Each of our concerns and how we internalize and handle them are different as well. Some people might feel an immediate relief and a sense of overcoming the subject of their affirmation. For others, the changes may be gradual. The important part is to persevere in your tapping practice.

If you intend to use tapping to overcome more than one issue, the time needed might differ for concern A versus concern B. Along the way, you might even discover that what you thought was causing a negative emotion or reaction wasn't really the true cause. It was something entirely different that you had to spend time working to find out. That is okay, too. In fact, learning something like this creates instant awareness and the ability to focus on the correct thing immediately.

What's important to remember is that changes and improvements *do* happen. Be pleasantly surprised if you feel positive changes right from the start, but don't give up if this doesn't happen.

Part of what makes tapping such a great proactive "health giver" and so successful is that unlike many other regimens, maintenance is easy. If you tap twice a day (or however often you feel is best for you), keep it up even when you feel fantastic. Keeping your energy flowing is the intent, and it requires regular maintenance. The fact that it takes only a short session each day to accomplish makes it well worth the investment. It is far better to stay healthy this way, rather than to get healthy, slack off, and then wait until you hurt before you are motivated to try fixing yourself once again. The latter is like struggling to adopt an extreme diet and exercise routine to get in shape for a wedding or other occasional event—it's much better just to embrace good practices year-round. The same is true of tapping. Once you have healed, maintenance is paramount to continued success.

Q: I'd like to lose a few pounds. How does tapping help with weight loss?

A: You have gained weight for one of a few reasons, any or all of which can be related. You are overeating, your diet consists primarily of unhealthy foods (i.e., junk food), you are inactive, or there is a medical reason, such as diabetes or thyroid problems.

If you are talking about a few pounds put on over a gradual span of time, the odds are your eating and exercise habits are to blame. If you are gaining weight rapidly but honestly have a mostly healthy diet and are doing some regular exercise, see your physician to get your blood tested for early diabetes or other concerns. In all of the preceding scenarios, tapping can help, but you need to know the reason to address your weight gain.

Most often (including in the case of diabetes or other medical issues), the real root is emotional (refer to the sections on weight management and diabetes earlier in this book). If you have negative feelings impacting you on a consistent basis, your immune system is not functioning at its best. Of course, feeling sad or frustrated does not directly cause you to get a disease, but the negative emotions do prohibit your body's natural flow of healthy and restorative energy, which can lead to physical manifestations.

Once you have determined what has caused your weight gain, write out your "I Want to Eliminate" and "I Want to Achieve" lists, create your personalized affirmation, and start tapping.

Q: I have a lot of fear in expressing my emotions. What's the best way for me to begin the process?

A: Playact! Kids use this term when playing a game of make-believe. Step outside of yourself and disassociate in a way. Look at yourself and really analyze your situation—but not from the perspective of you as the person feeling sadness, pain, or frustration. Rather, pretend you are a caring friend or acquaintance, and think of ways you could change or be helped. You are not going to be that unhappy person forever, so it really is easier than it sounds.

Labeling your fear with the correct name is something only you will ever know. There is absolutely no one to pass judgment on your fear or your expression of an emotion. Sometimes it is easier to whisper the word that represents your fear. Do that, and do it a bunch of times. You'll find your voice getting slightly louder after the first few whispers. Keep at it. You will find yourself saying "the word" aloud and then perhaps even hollering it.

What you have really done is acknowledged what was bothering you; that is the start of removing it from your life. Incorporate the fear into a tapping routine, and work to keep that negativity out for good.

Q: What should I do if I have physical pain after a tapping session?

A: You should not be experiencing pain from the act of tapping itself, because it is a gentle, natural practice. Instead, the sensation of pain is usually due to that negative emotion being brought to light and acknowledged. It is not necessarily a common occurrence, but it is both normal and understandable.

If your mind had buried an unhappy memory, but suddenly that memory becomes laid bare and right out there for you to see, pain is a natural reaction. One example is the realization and acknowledgment of sexual or emotional abuse as a young child that surface while you're tapping to address what you thought was an entirely different issue. You just got hit with a zinger. You went from years of absolutely zero recognition of a highly traumatic event to full immersion in this past occurrence. Frankly, if you didn't feel pain—emotional, mental, physical, or possibly all three—something would be wrong.

Pain is never a welcome sensation. However, in a case like this, it is a positive step. Knowing the primary reason, the underlying reason, for whatever is wrong or "off" within you is the start of healing. You have just taken an extraordinary step on your own behalf. With acknowledgment of the pain and the reason for it, you are well on the road to full recovery and a much happier life.

Q: What do I do if I have a negative emotional reaction to tapping?

A: Many of the reasons for experiencing a negative emotional reaction after tapping are the same as for experiencing a painful physical reaction. As you discover the reason—the true underlying cause—for whatever is bothering you, causing blockages and negative energy, your system is sent reeling. For many people, that negative emotional reaction, if experienced, is due to letting go of something that has been a part of their life for years. There is an immediate sense of loss, emptiness, and lack of completeness. This holds true even when the loss is of something that was making you miserable.

In a way, giving up what was making you unhappy or unhealthy is like putting an end to an addiction. Immediate withdrawal can shock the system. You feel bereft. Ridding yourself of destructive and negative emotions can cause a feeling of loss. It doesn't last long—perhaps only a few seconds, perhaps several days—but the key is that you understand why and can swiftly address it. The best and fastest way to accept and resolve that moment of negativity is to acknowledge it. Then you can smile and wave good-bye to whatever it was causing havoc in your life.

Q: I feel self-conscious while tapping. How can I get over that?

A: Until you are accustomed to tapping, you may want to do it in the privacy of your bedroom or in the bathroom. In fact, you can even tap while in the shower. Assuming you've already determined what your affirmation will be and know what you'd like to address, the entire preparation and sequence takes no more than five to ten minutes at most. That includes going through the full sequence a few times.

By the way, feeling self-conscious about tapping is quite common and not at all surprising. You are doing something new, something a bit different from what you are accustomed to, and you're interacting with your physical body in a unique, visible way as well as addressing sometimes uncomfortable emotions. Remember when you first sat behind the steering wheel when you learned to drive? You were excited but very self-conscious and worried about perhaps driving on the wrong side of the road or hitting the car at the end of the block. Tapping, like anything new, can make you uncomfortable or self-conscious at the start.

The best way to get over being self-conscious while tapping is to do it regularly. Practice makes everything easier, and the confidence you gain from your progress will be motivation enough. You'll feel more comfortable and at ease before you know it.

Q: I'm embarrassed to do tapping in public, but I travel a lot for work. Do you have any suggestions for continuing my practice outside my house?

A: Absolutely! Bathrooms are a great idea when it comes to a few minutes of alone time. That includes airplane restrooms also. If your company has you overnighting when on business travel, your hotel room should offer the needed privacy as well.

It is totally okay to eliminate tapping along your side (Point 8) if you are in public. When on a plane or train, if you want to tap—for example, for overcoming fear of flying or fear of public places—doing so as often as needed is an instant help. You can simply use the quick version. Even just a minute or two of tapping and deep breathing will work wonders. Breathe deeply and slowly while tapping just your hand—you can use a book, magazine, jacket, or purse to cover what you're doing if need be. Tapping by your eyes is evocative of what many people do while thinking anyway—and the same is true when tapping on the indentation between your nose and lip and between your lip and chin, as well as for your tender spot. If you don't act embarrassed, no one will ever have a clue what you are really doing, and who knows, your calm demeanor afterward might even intrigue them enough to want to learn about tapping.

Q: What do I tell people about tapping if they are curious and ask?

A: Whatever you are comfortable telling them! You can explain the process in full or simply refer them to a few sources of information. As with anything, each person should do some personal research based on why he or she might be interested in tapping and verify that it's right for him or her. "To tap or not to tap" is an individual decision.

Q: I'd like my boyfriend to give tapping a try to help us with some relationship problems, but he's not into it. What should I do?

A: As much as you might like to make tapping a mutually beneficial practice for the two of you, you should not—and cannot—force someone else to do something he is not interested in pursuing. You can only hope to lead by example.

If your boyfriend sees you becoming happier and healthier, that may well be the motivation he needs to follow suit. You can only do what is best for you. If he's not in the right frame of mind for tapping, it won't be successful, and that defeats the purpose. As with any intent to work together to solve relationship problems, it won't be effective unless both parties are willing and engaged participants. So don't feel guilty, irritated, or frustrated. Just take care of you. Continue tapping and sing its praises. A happier, healthier you is the best carrot you can ever dangle.

Q: What if I don't have any serious emotional or physical issues I need to address with tapping?

A: Be appreciative and tap for ongoing health and happiness maintenance. Remember the analogy early in this book about only seeing a chiropractor for the first time when your back or neck pain became unbearable and truly scary? Once your spinal alignment is corrected, then you should visit the chiropractor for maintenance. Tapping is exactly the same.

Tapping on a regular basis is health maintenance of your emotional, psychological, and physical well-being. Tapping keeps your energy flowing properly and your meridians unblocked. Positive energy and optimal body functioning are the results. Just a few minutes every day means tapping is the best investment in yourself that you can make.

Q: What do I do if I don't see any immediate results from tapping?

A: Keep at your tapping practice! You don't get sick overnight, nor do you wake up one morning and decide you are severely depressed. Problems build up over time. It is no different than a blocked artery: one bite of rich food didn't transform a healthy artery to a clogged one. Accumulation of unhealthy foods ingested over years led to that blockage. Addressing and fixing your illness takes time as well.

Your mental and emotional health is exactly the same as your physical health. If, for example, you suffer from panic attacks, you now know there is an underlying negative emotion for them. Your affirmation is to acknowledge and accept yourself—panic attacks and all—but you also want to get rid of them.

Step 1 is recognizing and accepting that the panic attacks exist. Step 2 is your active decision to banish them from your life. Step 3 is the process of eliminating them, preventing them from being an intuitive reaction by calmly resolving each situation in which they occur.

Some people experience an almost instantaneous change with tapping, but not everyone does. Success comes, but you have to apply yourself to find success. Even those of you who experience immediate and total relief from whatever ails you need to keep up daily maintenance. So consider a less immediate "cure" as part of your maintenance process. What matters is that improvement does happen—and it will in time.

Q: How often should I tap?

A: To some extent, this depends on what you are trying to oust from your life. Dealing with addictions requires more daily tapping than many other issues because the urge to use the addictive substance is both physical and mental. Addictions aside, tapping should ideally be done twice a day: in the morning within a reasonable time of rising, and in the evening before going to bed. This is for basic maintenance.

If you feel the urge to tap at other times throughout the day, your body is telling you something. So go ahead and make your system happy. Tap whenever you feel the urge. That urge might just be a precursor to a need.

Q: I'm quite elderly—far past 65. Is it too late for me to begin tapping?

A: You are never too old to begin tapping. In fact, there are more than a few pluses that come with age: from experience and wisdom, to the fact that older people often have more courage to honestly and analytically appraise what could use correcting in their life or body. Age brings clarity, and with clarity comes the ability to focus immediately on what you want to address. However, as has been stated throughout this book, do not stop taking any medications you might be on without speaking with your doctor first. Other than that, here's to age, wisdom, grace, and improved health and happiness!

Q: If I tap to help get rid of something, do I need to tap for that reason for the rest of my life after the problem is gone?

A: For optimal health and happiness, it would be a very good idea, if for no other reason than it was an issue once and could become one again. You do not *have* to do anything. Do whatever makes you feel good and keeps you happy. But remember that tapping is both curative and a maintenance program, so at least occasionally acknowledging that issue to keep it "gone" might be worthwhile. The decision is entirely yours, so trust your needs.

Q: Can tapping benefit me? How?

A: Read, or reread as the case may be, this book to make that decision for yourself. Do outside research to supplement your knowledge and understanding of the tapping process. Consider seeing a tapping practitioner if you are unsure. Take a few days to practice a routine and get familiar with how it fits into your life and makes you feel.

Tapping has helped countless people. Tapping does not require you to become a lifelong devotee, nor does it require you to believe in miracles. It's merely a technique for introducing positive energy into your life and eliminating the negative. Hopefully, this book has helped you discover how tapping would be beneficial for a healthier, happier you!

GLOSSARY

Acupressure: Acupressure is a modern-day derivative of acupuncture. Both are holistic, but rather than stimulating the meridian points with needles, acupressurists use their fingertips. This, in turn, clears blockages so energy can travel freely throughout the body and brain.

Acupuncture: Developed in China 5,000 years ago, and refined continuously since, acupuncture is a holistic form of medicine that uses the insertion of ultra-thin needles as the means of stimulating and unblocking meridians to allow a person's energy to flow freely and naturally in an effort to cure disease and relieve pain. Stimulating the meridians that are closest to the skin's surface results in reactivating the normal flow of positive energy to the brain.

Addiction: The term *addiction* is used most often as it relates to a person's dependency on chemical compounds or other substances that are used to rev up or slow down the natural flow of the body and thought processes. People can be addicted to drugs (prescription and over-the-counter), alcohol, caffeine, tobacco, sodas, and sweets, as well as other substances such as salt. Obviously some addictions are more severe than others, but addiction, in the true sense of the word, connotes a physical and mental need for and dependency on a habit-forming substance. Many, if not most, addicts have some form of withdrawal symptoms or side effects when the addictive substance is not used.

Affirmation: As used in tapping, an affirmation is your acknowledgment or statement of a concern or fear you want to eliminate. It is the written and oral statement that lays the groundwork for your tapping routine. You acknowledge and accept your concern without casting blame, fault, or anger.

Allergy: An allergy is a physical reaction or hypersensitivity to something. Common allergies can range from cat dander, to flower pollen, to bee venom, and the degree of reaction differs with the individual and is based on the buildup and intensity of the cause. Allergies to chemicals are also fairly common and run the gamut from smog to fragrances to manufactured compounds used in everything from laundry detergent to vaccines and medications. Allergies are by and large not inherited, and allergic reactions range from a mild rash to death.

Alternative medicine: Alternative medicine is the nomenclature used for all forms of medical treatment that fall outside the confines of Western medicine as we know it. What is considered alternative medicine in the United States is considered standard practice in other countries; perfect examples include acupuncture, chiropractic, massage therapy, and herbal medicine. All of these practices are standard noninvasive medical treatments in many other countries. Throughout much of Europe, Canada, Australia, and New Zealand, a more equal inclusion of alternative medicine in everyday care is the norm. Alternative medicine is usually holistic in nature and is slowly establishing its place alongside Western medicine in the United States.

Anxiety: Anxiety, while similar to stress, is more acute in its expression and manifestation. Where stress might make you want to scream, stamp your foot, or grind your teeth in anger or frustration, anxiety can often include extreme tension, a racing pulse, and profuse perspiration. It can also lead to panic attacks as well as confusion between the real and the imagined or perceived. Stress can be a precursor to anxiety, which often manifests as an inability to cope with situations.

Chiropractic: Chiropractic medicine or therapy deals primarily with the spine and the vertebrae. Keeping the spine properly aligned to allow for full and healthy body movement and function is the overall aim.

Depression: Depression, like anxiety, has a more serious meaning in medical terms than in daily language. "I'm depressed about my boyfriend or my job," is a far cry from the clinical use of the term *depression*. In this book, *depression* is used to indicate a medical or psychological concern. Depression can be a psychological or neurological disorder that manifests itself through loss of sleep or insomnia; lack of vitality and energy; eating disorders; difficulty thinking or concentrating; and extreme sadness and withdrawing from people. Worst-case scenarios for depression include suicidal tendencies or destructive actions.

Disease: Disease is a negative condition in one or multiple parts of one's body that makes us unable to function as we should. Disease runs the spectrum from the common cold to severely debilitating diseases such as diabetes, multiple sclerosis, kidney failure, and cancer. The optimal way to fight diseases of all kinds is to keep our immune system functioning at its peak.

Disorder: A medical or psychological disorder is an abnormal physical or mental condition.

Endorphin: Endorphins are what make you feel good after an hour of exercising. They are proteins that occur in the brain and are released into the body through the nervous system (along with serotonin) after exertion, as well as in response to pain. The study of endorphins is still somewhat in the early stages, but scientists believe that the stimulation and release of endorphins can possibly play a role in treating chronic pain, among other things.

Energy: Energy is the fundamental basis of our ability to function and perform as living things. Our energy level is directly reflective of the extent of our ability to be active physically and mentally. When we feel good, we have tons of energy; when we are sick or feeling down, our energy level plummets. As energy relates to tapping, it is the key element in helping us achieve our intentions or affirmations. When positive healing energy can flow freely and correctly throughout the human body's system, it keeps the immune system functioning and counteracts communicable diseases as well as stress.

Holistic medicine: Holistic medicine is an alternative form of medicine that approaches health from a whole system view. Holistic medicine addresses your complete self as opposed to any single part of you. Both the body and the mind are viewed as one entity that cannot be separated, as each has an impact on the well-being of the other.

Meditation: Meditation is quiet time. Meditation techniques use both concentration and contemplation, even though your mind becomes more or less blank as it wanders and rests. The use of a word or sound—often called a mantra ("om" is a standard one)—helps focus the mind and allows you to leave worries and cares behind for a time. The greatest benefit of meditation is peacefulness and letting go. The result is a clearer mind and an increased ability to achieve what you want. Meditation, as many practice it, has absolutely no religious overtones or requirements, although the practice is part of both Hinduism and Buddhism.

Meridian: The meridians are the pathways (or roads) that energy travels along between various parts of the body and the correlating segments of the brain. A person's inherent electrical energy must get where it needs to go to do its job, which is to keep the person healthy and positive, and it follows the meridian lines to accomplish this.

Pain: Pain is a negative state of being. It can be physical, emotional, mental, or a combination of all three. Pain can range from mildly uncomfortable to unbearably agonizing. When in constant or severe pain, all aspects of life are adversely impacted. Chronic pain can be greatly debilitating. When a peron is in pain, nothing works correctly; the body is preoccupied trying to deal with the pain rather than focusing on other healthy functions.

Phobia: Phobias are categorized exaggerated fears that are often illogical, but very real, possibly all-consuming, and terrifying. Phobias are frequently disabling and are based in anxiety disorders.

Post-traumatic stress disorder (PTSD): PTSD has become a growing issue and concern in recent decades as military personnel—suffering from what used to be called "battle fatigue" but is now more correctly addressed and treated as PTSD—have returned from active duty. PTSD does not have to be combat related, however. PTSD can affect anyone following a traumatic accident, suffering a severe emotional loss, surviving a devastating flood or earthquake, and so on. Simply stated, PTSD is a psychological reaction to a high-stress situation; it is emotionally based—the mind cannot handle the shock, horror, or stress.

Serotonin: Serotonin is the other half of why endorphins can make you feel so on top of the world naturally. The endorphins raise your serotonin level, and the release of both into your bloodstream creates a natural high.

Stress: Stress is the source of most of our aches, ailments, and woes mentally, emotionally, and physically. Stress causes tension; tension and fraught nerves wreak havoc on our health and well-being. Learning to diffuse the stress in your life is the fastest, most effective, and longest-lasting road to happiness and health.

Yoga: Yoga is a form of exercise focused on stretching, muscle control, and deep breathing. While Hindu in origin, yoga does not require any form of religious belief or adherence. It combines the peacefulness of meditation and the accompanying deep breathing with elongating and strengthening every muscle in your body.

BIBLIOGRAPHY

Carrington, Patricia, PhD, "History of Meridian Tapping and EFT"
Mastering the Practice of EFT and Meditation with Patricia Carrington, PhD, accessed June 7, 2013
http://masteringeft.com/masteringblog/about-eft/history-of-eft/

Craig, Gary, *The EFT Manual*
Santa Rosa, CA: Energy Psychology Press, 2011.

EFT, Emotional Freedom Techniques
EFTUniverse.com, accessed June 7, 2013
http://www.eftuniverse.com

Mayo Clinic, "Diseases and Conditions"
MayoClinic.com, accessed June 7, 2013
http://www.mayoclinic.com/health/DiseasesIndex/DiseasesIndex

Mayo Clinic, "Symptoms"
MayoClinic.com, accessed June 7, 2013
http://www.mayoclinic.com/health/symptoms/
SymptomIndex

Naik, Gautam, "Mistakes in Scientific Studies Surge"
Wall Street Journal, August 10, 2011
http://online.wsj.com/article/SB10001424052702303627 1
04576411850666582080.html

National Center for Complementary and Alternative Medicine (NCCAM)
Accessed June 7, 2013
http://nccam.nih.gov/

National Heart, Lung, and Blood Institute
Accessed June 7, 2013
http://www.nhlbi.nih.gov/

National Institute of Mental Health (NIMH)
Accessed June 7, 2013
http://www.nimh.nih.gov/index.shtml

National Institutes of Health (NIH)
Accessed June 7, 2013
http://www.nih.gov/

Niebuhr, Reinhold, "Serenity Prayer"
Accessed June 7, 2013
http://en.wikipedia.org/wiki/Serenity_Prayer

Rogers, Lisa, "EFT for PTSD/Trauma"
Center for Emotional Freedom, accessed June 7, 2013
http://www.centerforemotionalfreedom.com

Made in the USA
Lexington, KY
21 July 2014